DATE DUE

DEMCO, INC. 38-2931

Making Fleece Crafts

Written by Judy Ann Sadler
Illustrated by June Bradford

KIDS CAN PRESS

To all my warm, fuzzy nieces and nephews

Kids Can Press acknowledges the financial support of the Government of Canada, through the BPIDP, for our publishing activity.

Published in Canada by
Kids Can Press Ltd.
29 Birch Avenue
Toronto, ON M4V 1E2

Published in the U.S. by
Kids Can Press Ltd.
2250 Military Road
Tonawanda, NY 14150

www.kidscanpress.com

Edited by Laurie Wark
Designed by Karen Powers
Printed in Hong Kong by Wing King Tong Company Limited

The hardcover edition of this book is smyth sewn casebound.
The paperback edition of this book is limp sewn with a drawn-on cover.

CM   00 0 9 8 7 6 5 4 3 2
CM PA 00 0 9 8 7 6 5 4 3 2 1

Canadian Cataloguing in Publication Data

Sadler, Judy Ann, 1959 –
    Making fleece crafts

(Kids can do it)
ISBN 1-55074-847-5 (bound)   ISBN 1-55074-739-8 (pbk.)

1. Textile crafts — Juvenile literature. 2. Sewing — Juvenile literature.
3. Synthetic fabrics — Juvenile literature. I. Bradford, June. II. Title. III. Series.

TT712.S22 2000   j746   C99-932788-7

Kids Can Press is a Nelvana company

Contents

Introduction

How would you like to make your own funky fleece hats and fuzzy fleece neckwarmers? How about irresistible beanbag animals, cozy tuck-away blankets and fleecy throw-pillows to toss on your bed? All the projects in this book are designed to be made out of fleece. You may know it as Arctic fleece, Polarfleece, Polartec or other brand names. You'll be amazed at how easy fleece is to use, even if you've never sewn before. Some of these crafts can be glued together, while others don't need sewing or gluing. Fleece is warm, soft, stretchy, colorful, nonraveling, easy to wash, quick to dry and, best of all, simple to work with. You can make things to wear for school, camping and hiking, or for your room and for gift giving. The instructions, patterns, stitches and ideas are all here, so get busy!

MATERIALS

Fleece

This fabulous fabric is usually made of polyester, which is a manufactured fiber. Some fleece is even made from recycled plastic soda-pop bottles. Buy fleece at a fabric store in the amounts you need or look for remnants. Sometimes large end-of-the-roll pieces are available inexpensively. Use double-sided fleece for the projects in this book. It usually looks the same front and back, but if one side looks or feels better, use it as the "right" side. The other side will be the "wrong" side. Fleece stretches more one way than the other. If this is important for the item you are making, the instructions will tell you how to find and position the stretchier side.

Fabric markers

Use erasable fabric markers to trace patterns or to make marks on light-colored fleece. Use a chalk pencil, dressmaker's marker or a sliver of dried soap for darker fleece. Don't use permanent markers because the ink might show through to the other side of the fleece.

Straight pins

It's a good idea to use pins with beads on the ends so they don't get lost in the fleece. Handle pins carefully and store them in a small container or pin cushion.

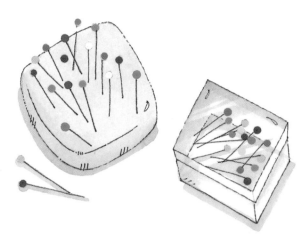

Needles, thread and embroidery floss

Use a sturdy needle and good-quality polyester thread that matches your fleece. Whenever you sew with embroidery floss, use a needle with a large eye.

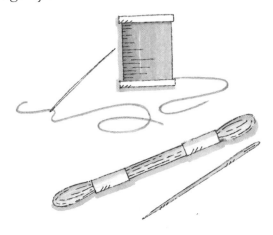

Permanent fabric glue

Some of the projects in this book can be glued rather than stitched together. Fabric glue can also be used for appliqué. Fabric glue is available at craft-supply and fabric stores. Follow the manufacturer's instructions.

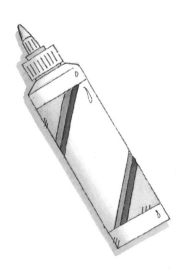

Basic sewing stitches

Refer to these pages whenever you need sewing information.

Threading a needle

Cut a piece of thread twice the length of your arm. Wet one end in your mouth and poke it through the eye of the needle. Or, use a needle threader by poking the wire loop into the eye, dropping the thread into the wire loop and pulling the wire and thread back through the eye. For embroidery floss, tightly pinch one end between your index finger and thumb as you push down into the floss with the eye of a large needle.

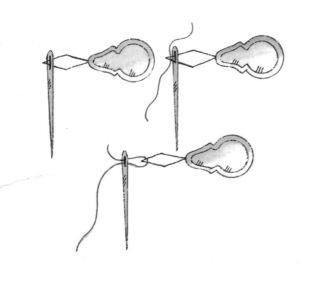

Knotting the thread

Double the thread so that the ends are even (except when using embroidery floss — then the ends should be different lengths). Lick your index finger and wind the thread ends around it once. Hold the thread with your thumb and roll it off your finger. Hold the ends and pull to make a knot.

Overcast stitch

1. With knotted thread in your needle, pull the needle through the fleece.

2. Bring the needle around the edge of the fleece and go in again from the same side as the first stitch, but a little way over. Keep stitching in this way.

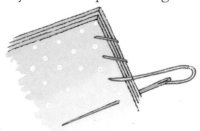

3. When you run out of thread or reach the end, make two or three small stitches on top of or near the last stitch and cut the thread.

Backstitch

If you have a sewing machine, it can be used when the instructions call for the backstitch. Always ask an adult to help you with a sewing machine.

1. With doubled, knotted thread in your needle, bring the needle up through the fleece about 0.5 cm (¼ in.) from the edge.

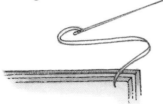

2. Poke the needle down through the fleece closer to the edge, then bring it back up a short distance from this first stitch.

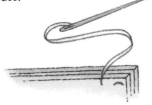

3. Poke the needle back down through the fleece in the same spot where you first poked the needle into the fabric. Keep the stitches small and even and close to the edge of the fleece.

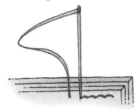

4. When you run out of thread or reach the end, make two or three small stitches on top of or near the last stitch and cut the thread.

Blanket stitch

1. With knotted embroidery floss in your needle, bring the needle through the fleece from the back to the front.

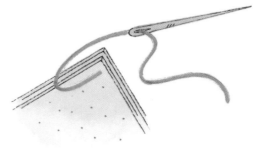

2. Poke the needle into the fleece from the front to the back this time, about 1 cm (½ in.) over from where you just came out.

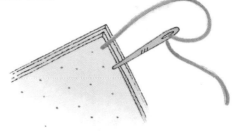

3. Pull the floss through the fleece as shown, with the floss behind the needle. Poke the needle in from the front to the back again and continue in this way. The first stitch will likely be slanted, but the rest will be straight.

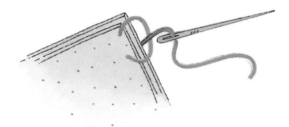

4. When you run out of floss or reach the end, knot and cut the floss.

No-sew scarf

This easy-to-make scarf is extra wide for warmth, but you can cut it narrower if you like. When you wear your scarf, be sure to tuck the ends into your coat.

YOU WILL NEED

- a measuring tape or ruler
- fleece
- scissors
- a fabric marker

1 Cut a strip of fleece about 140 cm x 30 cm (55 in. x 12 in.).

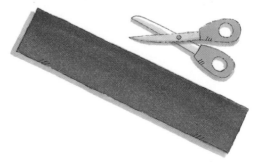

2 Draw a line across each end, about 8 cm (3 in.) in from the edge.

3 Make the fringe by cutting slits along the edge, about 1 cm (½ in.) apart, to the line on each end of the scarf. Wipe away the marked line.

Snake scarf

To wear this scarf, simply pull the snake tail through the slits and snug the scarf around your neck. Be sure to keep the ends tucked into your coat.

YOU WILL NEED

- a measuring tape or ruler
- fleece • scissors
- supplies for appliqué (see page 34 or 35) or dimensional fabric paint

1 Cut a strip of fleece about 120 cm x 20 cm (47 in. x 8 in.). Cut one end into a snake's head and the other into a tail.

2 Make two 5 cm (2 in.) lengthwise slits about 3 cm (1¼ in.) apart, 35 cm (14 in.) from the head end.

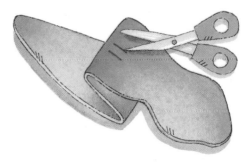

3 Decorate your scarf with eyes and markings using appliqué (see page 34 or 35) or dimensional fabric paint. If you like, stitch on a tongue.

Snuggly neckwarmer

Just pull this neckwarmer over your head and it'll keep you cozy. It can be stitched or glued together.

YOU WILL NEED

- a measuring tape or ruler
- fleece
- a fabric marker • scissors
- pins, a needle and thread or permanent fabric glue
- a large needle and embroidery floss (optional)

1 Use the fabric marker to draw a 55 cm (22 in.) square of fleece, and cut it out.

2 Pull the square in both directions to find out which way is stretchier. Fold it in half, right sides together (if your fleece has a right and wrong side), so the short ends are stretchier than the long sides.

3 If you are sewing the neckwarmer, pin and stitch the long side using a backstitch or overcast stitch (see pages 6–7). Remove the pins as you sew.

If you are gluing the neckwarmer, run a line of glue along both long edges. Let the glue set for a couple of minutes (or follow the manufacturer's instructions). Then lightly press the glued edges together. Allow the glue to dry.

4 Start turning the neckwarmer inside out but only go halfway. You should not be able to see your stitching (or the glued seam) and the stretchy ends should be together.

5 If you are sewing your neckwarmer, use a loose overcast stitch or blanket stitch (see pages 6–7) to sew the layered ends together.

If you are using glue, dab it between the layers. (Don't use a solid line of glue as it will not stretch as much as the fabric does.) Allow the glue to dry.

Cozy headband

Whether you're making this headband for yourself or someone else, the instructions will tell you how to adjust the size.

YOU WILL NEED

- fleece
- a measuring tape or ruler
- a fabric marker
- pins, a needle and thread or permanent fabric glue
- a large safety pin

1 Pull your fleece in both directions to find out which way is stretchier. Along the stretchy side, cut a length of fleece 55 cm x 18 cm (22 in. x 7 in.).

2 Fold the fabric in half lengthwise with the right sides together (if your fleece has a right and wrong side).

3 If you are sewing the headband together, pin and stitch the long side using a backstitch or an overcast stitch (see pages 6–7). Remove the pins as you sew.

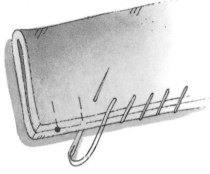

If you are gluing the headband together, run a line of glue on each long side and press the edges together. Allow the glue to dry.

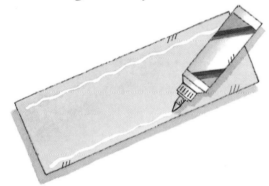

4 Fasten the safety pin to the seam area of one end. Tuck it into the fleece tube and work it through to the other end to turn the headband right side out. Remove the pin.

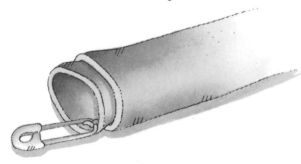

5 Try it on. Hold the ends together so that it fits snugly. Slip it off and mark the spot where the ends overlap.

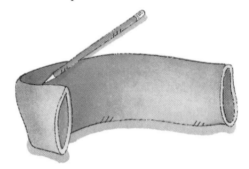

6 Tuck one end of the headband into the other, up to the marked line. If you are sewing it together, use an overcast stitch (see page 6).

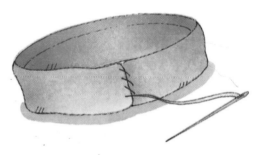

If you are gluing it, run a line of glue all around the tucked-in area.

OTHER IDEAS

Decorate your headband with appliqué (see page 34 or 35) or a few buttons.

Pom-pom hat

You will have enough fabric left over after making this hat to also make a neckwarmer, mittens or other crafts in this book.

YOU WILL NEED

- 0.7 m (¾ yd.) of fleece
- a measuring tape or ruler
- a fabric marker • scissors
- pins, a needle and thread or permanent fabric glue
- a 50 cm x 2.5 cm (20 in. x 1 in.) strip of fleece in a different color
- beads with large holes such as pony beads

1 Pull the fleece in both directions to find out which way is stretchier. Cut a rectangle of fleece that is 55 cm (22 in.) wide on the stretchy end and 70 cm (28 in.) long the other way.

2 Fold it in half lengthwise with the right sides together (if your fleece has a right and wrong side).

3 If you are sewing, pin and stitch the long side using an overcast stitch (see page 6) or a running stitch as shown. Remove the pins as you sew.

If you are gluing, run a line of glue along each long side and press the edges together. Allow the glue to dry.

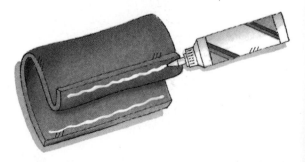

4 Start turning the hat right side out, but only go halfway. You should not be able to see the stitched (or glued) seam.

5 Gather the top of the hat (the unfinished end) in one hand. Adjust the gathered area until it looks like a flower.

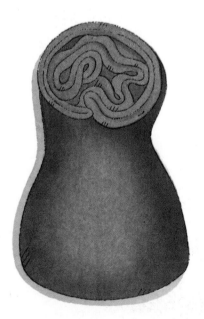

6 Tightly knot the strip of fleece about 5 cm (2 in.) down from the top of the hat. Thread some beads onto the ties and knot the ends to hold the beads in place.

7 Cut the top into short strips, being careful not to snip the hat.

8 Try on your new hat and adjust the brim until the hat fits just right.

Dino-mite hat

Try making this playful hat from three bold colors of fleece. To add a tassel, see page 32.

YOU WILL NEED

- 2 different-colored pieces of fleece, each 60 cm (24 in.) square
- a 50 cm x 7 cm (20 in. x 2¾ in.) strip of fleece in a third color
- a measuring tape or ruler
- a fabric marker
- scissors
- pins, a needle and thread
- a large needle and embroidery floss

1 Cut spikes into one long side of the strip of fleece. Don't cut them too deep. Set this piece aside.

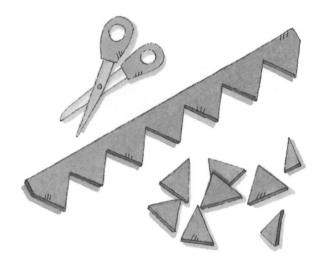

2 Pull one square of fleece in both directions to find out which way is stretchier. Fold it in half so that the short ends are stretchier than the long sides. Pin along the long open side.

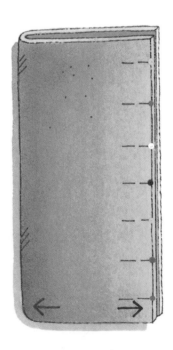

3 Measure 14 cm (5 ½ in.) from the folded corner along the bottom and make a dot, as shown. Make another dot 56 cm (22 in.) straight up on the fold. Join the dots.

4 Cut the fleece along the marked line and unfold the long triangle.

5 Repeat steps 2 to 4 with the other color of fleece. Place the triangles right sides together (if your fleece has a right and wrong side) and pin one long side. Sew them together using a backstitch or an overcast stitch (see pages 6–7). Remove the pins.

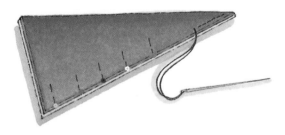

6 Open the hat and center the spikes along one long, unfinished side so they face inward.

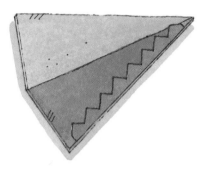

7 Close the hat so all three unfinished edges are even. Pin and overcast stitch or backstitch this long side. Remove the pins.

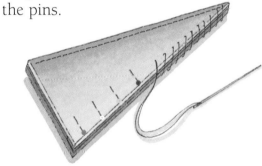

8 Turn the hat right side out. Turn and pin under about 1 cm (½ in.) of the bottom edge. Blanket-stitch (see page 7) it in place and remove the pins as you sew.

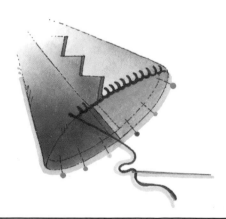

Jester hat

Make this colorful, jingling jester hat for fun and warmth.

YOU WILL NEED

- a pencil, paper, scissors and tape
- 2 different-colored pieces of fleece, each 70 cm (28 in.) square
- pins, a needle and thread
- 3 jingle bells

1 Trace the pattern pieces on pages 36–37 and cut them out. Tape them together as shown.

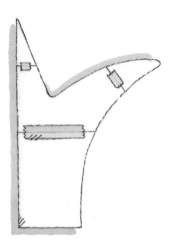

2 Pull one square of fleece in both directions to find out which way is stretchier. Fold it in half so that the short ends are stretchier than the long sides. Pin along the long, open side.

3 Pin the pattern so the long, straight side is along the fold of your fleece. Cut it out.

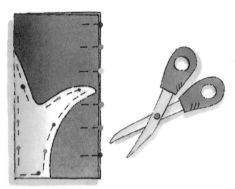

4 Remove the pattern and repeat steps 2 to 4 with the other fleece square. Open both halves of the hat and pin them right sides together. Use a backstitch (see page 7) around the three points. Leave the bottom open.

5 Turn up the bottom edge about 5 cm (2 in.) and pin it. Stitch the hem as shown. Remove the pins.

6 Clip the curves and corners of your hat and turn it right side out. Poke out the corners with a closed pair of scissors.

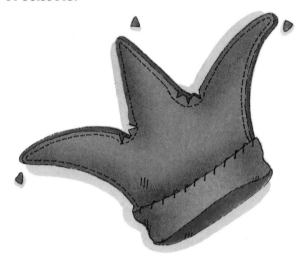

7 Stitch a bell on each point, try on your hat and jingle all the way!

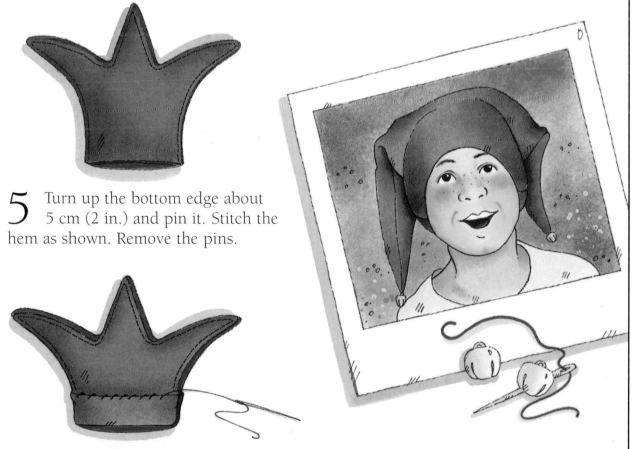

Two-color mittens

These reversible mittens also look great made from one plain piece of fleece and one printed piece.

YOU WILL NEED

- a pencil, paper, scissors, thin cardboard and white craft glue
- 2 colors of fleece • a fabric marker
- a needle and thread
- a large needle and embroidery floss

1 Place your hand on the paper with your fingers slightly apart and your thumb sticking straight out. (You may need to tape on another sheet of paper for length.) Starting and finishing halfway to your elbow, trace around your hand.

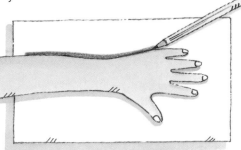

2 Lift your hand. Draw around your traced hand to make it larger, as shown, especially in the wrist area. Add 1 cm (½ in.) all around for a seam.

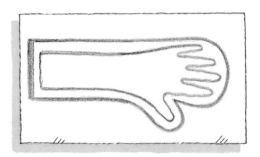

3 Cut out your paper pattern and glue it onto the cardboard. Cut it out again.

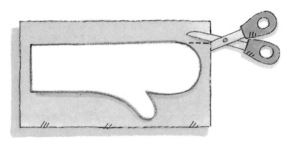

4 Trace the mitten shape four times on each color of fleece. (If your fleece has a right side, draw two shapes, flip the pattern over and draw two more. Do this for both colors.) Cut out all eight shapes.

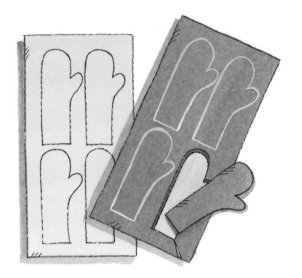

5 With right sides facing, pair and pin the shapes together. You should have two pairs of each colour. Sew around each mitten using a backstitch or an overcast stitch (see pages 6–7). Leave the bottoms open. Remove the pins.

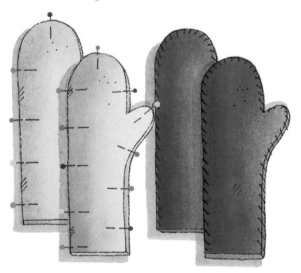

6 Turn only the two mittens of the first color right side out. Put a mitten of the second color on your hand and pull the first mitten on top. Smooth them together. Double the other two mittens the same way.

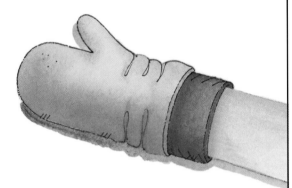

7 With the bottom edges even, pin and blanket-stitch (see page 7) around them. Remove the pins.

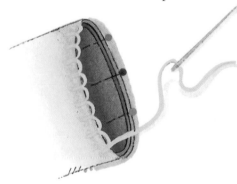

8 When you wear these mittens, turn up the cuff to show the other fabric. Turn them inside out when you want the other fleece to show.

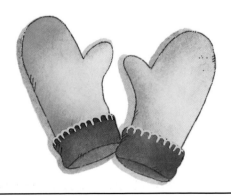

Slouchy slipper socks

These one-size-fits-most slippers are comfy and cozy, and the fabric paint makes them nonslip.

YOU WILL NEED

- fleece
- a measuring tape or ruler
- scissors   • a fabric marker
- pins, a needle and thread
- dimensional fabric paints

1 Pull your fleece in both directions to find out which way is stretchier. Cut two rectangles that are 30 cm (12 in.) wide on the stretchy end and 55 cm (22 in.) long the other way. Put one rectangle aside.

2 Fold and pin the fleece in half lengthwise so the wrong sides are together (if your fleece has a right and wrong side).

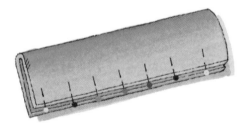

3 Backstitch, overcast stitch or blanket-stitch (see pages 6–7) this long seam. Remove the pins.

4 Place the slipper on a table so that the seam is down the center. Pin one end closed and round it off with the fabric marker to look like the toe area of a slipper.

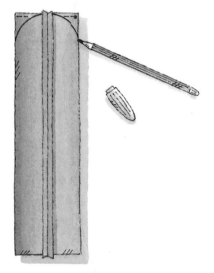

5 Cut along your marked area. Remove the pins from the scraps. Pin the toe area together and stitch it closed.

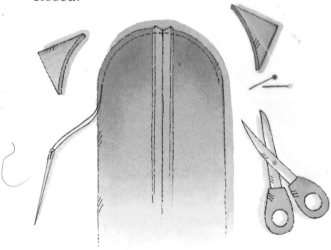

6 Follow steps 2 to 5 to make the other slipper.

7 Decorate the bottom of each slipper with the fabric paint and let them dry. If you like, you can decorate the fronts, too. Fold down the tops and try on your new slippers.

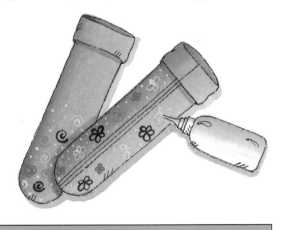

MORE IDEAS

• "Lace up" your slippers by making small holes on both sides of the front seam. Criss-cross the front using a strip of a different-colored fleece.

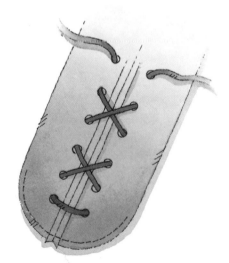

• Cut larger or smaller fleece rectangles to make slippers for super-big feet or teeny-tiny ones.

Beanbag pig

YOU WILL NEED

- a pencil, paper, scissors and thin cardboard
- white craft glue
- a piece of fleece about 25 cm x 40 cm (10 in. x 16 in.)
- a fabric marker
- pins, a needle and thread or embroidery floss
- plastic pellets (available at craft-supply stores) or dried beans
- an adult-sized sock
- dimensional fabric paint or a permanent fabric marker
- a two-hole button

1 Trace the pig pattern from page 38 and cut it out. Glue it onto the cardboard and cut it out again.

2 Trace the pattern twice onto the fleece. Cut both shapes out and mark one area to be left open.

3 Pin the pig shapes so that the wrong sides are together (if your fleece has a right and wrong side). Make sure all the edges are even.

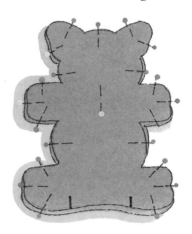

4 Backstitch, overcast stitch or blanket-stitch (see pages 6–7) around the pig, leaving the marked area open. Remove the pins as you sew.

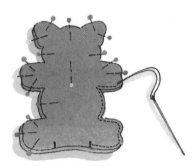

5 Pour pellets or beans into the opening. Continue stitching the pig until the opening is closed.

6 For the vest, cut off about 10 cm (4 in.) of ribbing from the sock. For armholes, cut slits 4 cm (1½ in.) long on each side, beginning about 2 cm (¾ in.) down from the top.

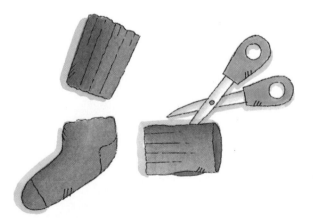

7 Slide the vest onto the pig. Roll down the neck and turn under the bottom.

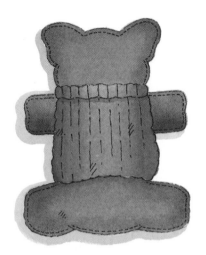

8 Paint or draw on hooves, eyes and a mouth. Glue on a button nose and curly fleece tail. Allow your pig to dry.

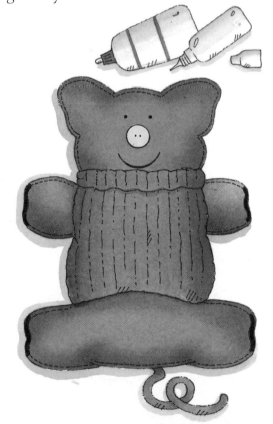

Fleecy frog

- a pencil, paper, scissors and thin cardboard
- white craft glue
- 2 different pieces of fleece, each 30 cm x 25 cm (12 in. x 10 in.)
- a fabric marker
- pins, a needle and thread or embroidery floss
- plastic pellets (available at craft-supply stores) or dried beans
- 2 small colorful pom-poms
- 2 medium-sized roly eyes

1 Trace the frog pattern from page 39 and cut it out. Glue it onto the cardboard and cut it out again.

2 Trace the frog pattern once onto each of the pieces of fleece. Cut them out. Mark one area to be left open.

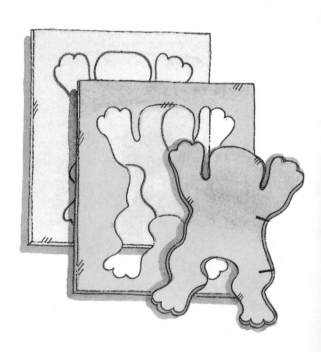

3 Pin the frog shapes so that the wrong sides are together (if your fleece has a right and wrong side), making sure all the edges are even.

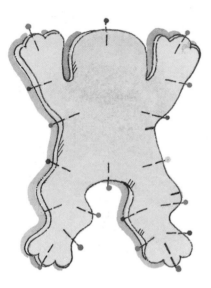

4 Backstitch, overcast stitch or blanket-stitch (see pages 6–7) around the frog, leaving the marked area open. Remove the pins as you sew.

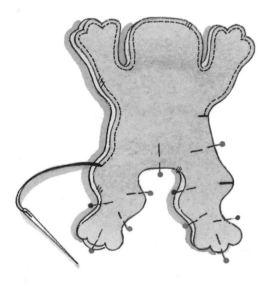

5 Pour pellets or beans into the opening until your frog can sit up. Continue stitching the frog until the opening is closed.

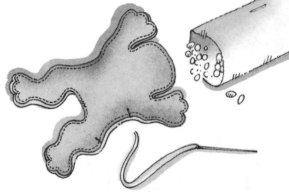

6 Glue the pom-poms onto your frog's head. Glue the roly eyes to the front of the pom-poms.

OTHER IDEAS

Give your frog a long, red-fleece tongue. Stitch it between the layers of fleece.

Blanket-in-a-pillow

This pillow transforms into a blanket. It's perfect for chilly evenings, camping trips and car rides. It also makes a terrific gift.

YOU WILL NEED

- 1.5 m (1⅔ yds.) of fleece
- a 40 cm (16 in.) square of fleece in the same or a contrasting color
- a large needle and embroidery floss or yarn
- pins, a needle and thread • scissors

1 Pull the small fleece square in both directions to find out which way is stretchier. With two arm lengths of embroidery floss, blanket-stitch (see page 7) one of the two less stretchy sides. If you like, you can also decorate the square with appliqué (see page 34 or 35).

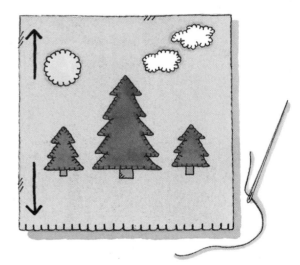

2 Spread out the large piece of fleece. Trim it so that there are no ragged edges. You may want to blanket-stitch all around it.

3 Pin the small square of fleece (appliquéd side down) in the top right-hand corner of the blanket, so that the blanket-stitched edge is placed as shown.

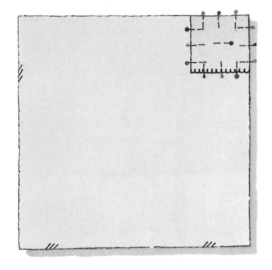

5 To tuck the blanket into the pocket, fold it in half four times. Make sure that each time you fold the blanket in half, the pocket is showing.

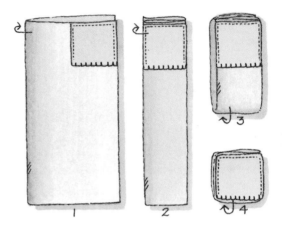

4 Backstitch (see page 7) up the right side, across the top and down the left side of the square. Leave the blanket-stitched edge open to form a pocket. Remove all the pins.

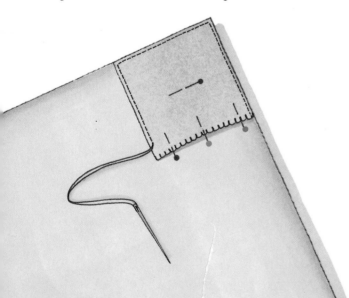

6 The blanket should now be the same size as the pocket. Turn the pocket inside out so that the blanket gets tucked into it. Smooth it and presto — a pillow!

More blankets

Here are more blanket ideas to keep you and your family, friends and pets, snug as bugs in rugs.

FRINGED BLANKET

On a plain or printed blanket-size piece of fleece, cut a fringe into opposite ends (see page 8). If you use plain fleece, you can decorate it with appliqué (see page 34 or 35) or dimensional fabric paint.

BABY PLAY BLANKET

Cut two pieces of colorful fleece, each about 1 m (1 yd.) square. Round all the corners. Pin and blanket-stitch (see page 7) the pieces together. Remove all the pins. When it is spread on the floor, this blanket makes a lovely, soft, washable play area for a baby. Don't decorate it in case a decoration falls off and becomes a choking hazard.

PET BLANKET

Fleece is a nice fabric for lining a cat or dog basket. Measure the length of the basket on the outside from the top of the side, across the bottom and up the other side. Measure the width in the same way. Use these measurements to cut a piece of fleece. Round off the corners. Use dimensional fabric paint to draw a cat or dog face in one corner with your pet's name above it. You can stitch it all around for a decorative touch.

HEARTY BLANKET

Fold a sheet of paper in half. Draw half a heart along the fold. Open it and use this as a pattern to cut out four fleece hearts. Appliqué (see pages 34 or 35) a heart onto each corner of a blanket-size piece of fleece in a contrasting color. Then cut out each corner to match the shape of the heart. You can blanket-stitch (see page 7) all around the blanket and appliqué on more hearts.

Tassel toss cushion

Use colorful scraps of fleece from other projects for the tassels on this toss cushion.

YOU WILL NEED

- 2 30 cm (12 in.) squares of fleece
- pins, a large needle and embroidery floss
- scissors
- polyester fiber stuffing
- colorful scraps of fleece
- a measuring tape or ruler
- a needle and thread

1   Pin the squares, wrong sides together. Blanket-stitch (see page 7) almost all the way around.

2   Stuff your cushion and finish stitching it closed.

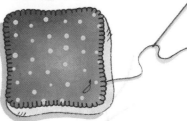

3   To make a tassel, cut six strips of fleece, each about 1 cm x 20 cm (½ in. x 8 in.). Place four strips together and tie them in the center with a fifth strip. Fold the five strips in half and knot them tightly with the sixth strip. Make three more tassels.

If you want curly tassels, cut the strips along the stretchy side of the fleece and make them only 0.5 cm (¼ in.) wide. Pull tightly on each strip end to curl it.

4   Stitch a tassel in each corner of your cushion.

Plenty of pillows

This method of making pillows allows lots of room for creativity.

1 Cut out a circle, heart, star, animal or other shape for your pillow. You could even do your name or initials in big balloon-style letters. Trace it on another piece of fleece and cut it out again.

2 You can decorate your pillow with appliqué (see page 34 or 35).

3 Pin your pillow shapes, wrong sides together. Blanket-stitch (see page 7) almost all the way around.

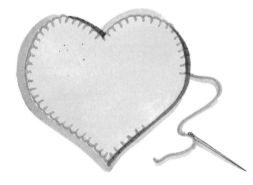

4 Stuff your pillow and finish stitching it closed.

Stitched appliqué

Appliqué is a terrific way to jazz up fleece items. See page 40 for some appliqué patterns to trace.

See page 40

YOU WILL NEED

- a fabric marker
- scraps of fleece
- scissors
- buttons or beads (optional)
- pins, a needle and embroidery floss

1 Draw a simple design on a scrap of fleece. Cut it out.

2 If you wish to add buttons or beads, stitch them on your appliqué design.

3 Pin the design to your fleece item. Sew all around the appliqué using the blanket stitch or the overcast stitch (see pages 6–7). Remove the pins.

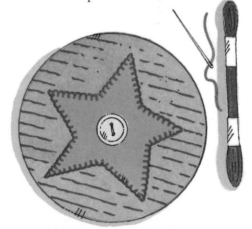

Iron-on appliqué

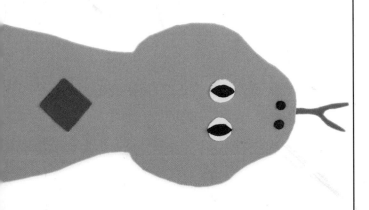

Here's a no-sew way to add appliqué designs to your fleece. You can also use fabric glue for smaller appliqué designs. (See page 40 for patterns.)

YOU WILL NEED

- fusible web, such as Pellon Wonder-Under (available at fabric stores)
  - scraps of fleece
    - an iron
    - a pencil
  - a damp pressing cloth

1 Place a piece of fusible web, paper side up (not the "rough" side) on a slightly larger piece of fleece.

2 Ask an adult to iron directly on the paper backing for three seconds to attach the web to the fleece (or follow the manufacturer's instructions). Let it cool.
Note: Fleece can melt if your iron is too hot. Use a medium-high setting and test on a scrap of fleece first.

3 Draw a simple design on the paper (draw letters backwards). Cut out your design.

4 Remove the paper backing and place this side down onto the fleece article. Cover with a damp cloth. Ask an adult to iron it for 10 seconds (or follow the manufacturer's instructions).

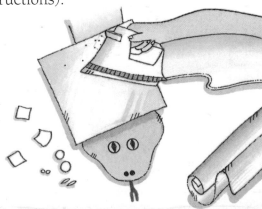

Jester hat pattern (for page 18)

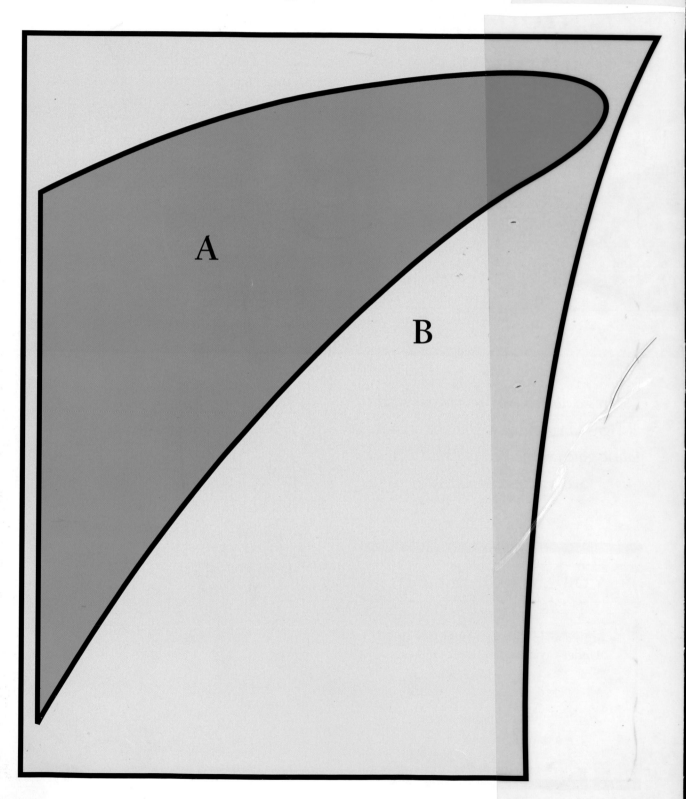

To make the pattern, trace the large pieces A, B, C and D onto paper. Cut out the traced pieces and tape them together as shown in the diagram on the right.

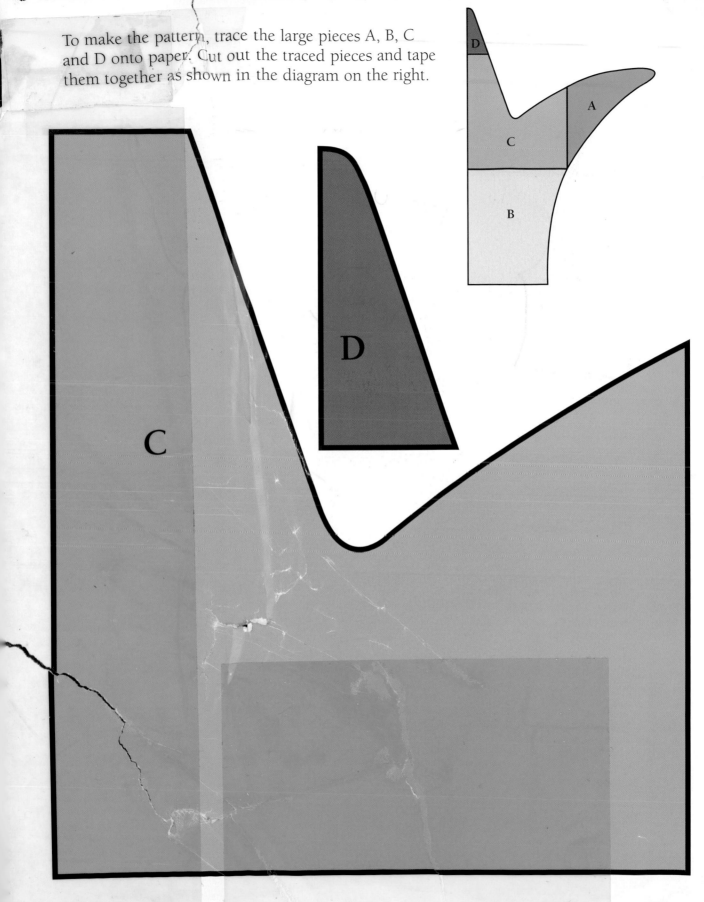

Beanbag pig pattern

(for page 24)

leave open

38

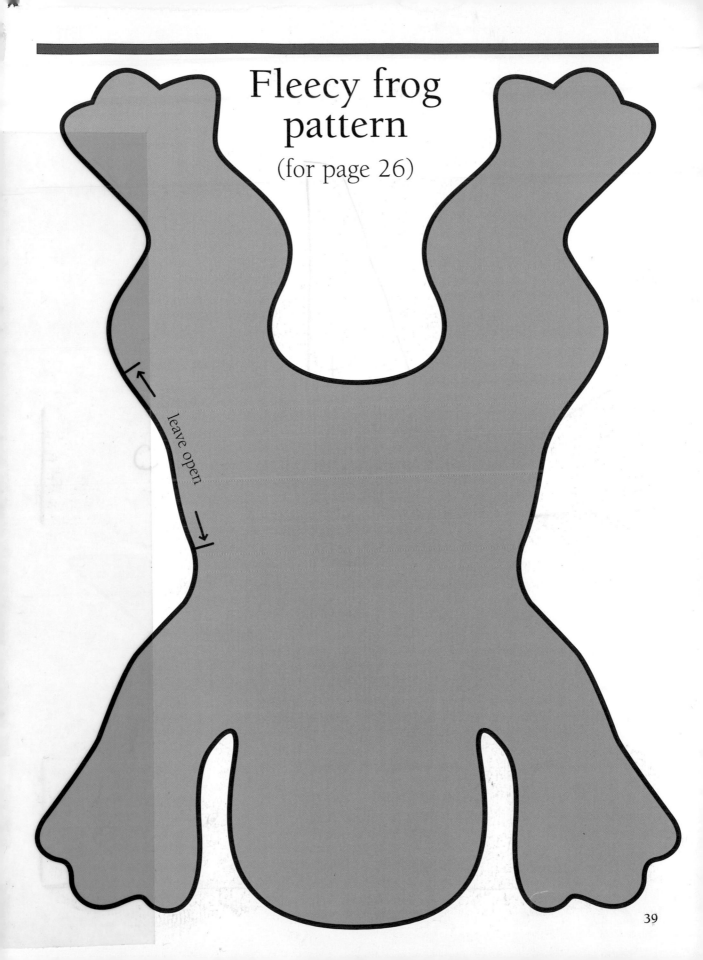

Fleecy frog pattern

(for page 26)

leave open

Appliqué patterns
(for pages 34–35)